THE LITTLE BOOK OF
TAROT

THE LITTLE BOOK OF TAROT

An Hachette UK Company
www.hachette.co.uk

Summersdale Publishers Ltd
Part of Octopus Publishing Group Limited
Carmelite House
50 Victoria Embankment
LONDON
EC4Y 0DZ
UK

www.summersdale.com

Printed and bound in China

ISBN: 978-1-78685-798-9

Substantial discounts on bulk quantities of Summersdale books are available to corporations, professional associations and other organizations. For details contact general enquiries: telephone: +44 (0) 1243 771107 or email: enquiries@summersdale.com.

THE LITTLE BOOK OF
TAROT

XANNA EVE CHOWN

summersdale

CONTENTS

6   **INTRODUCTION**

7   **PART 1: THE HISTORY OF TAROT**

11   **PART 2: THE CARDS**
13   The Major Arcana
63   The Minor Arcana

86   **PART 3: USING THE CARDS**
86   Choosing a deck
88   Energizing your new cards
88   Cleansing your cards
89   Getting to know the cards
91   Setting the scene
93   Setting your intention
94   Reading the cards
98   Tips for asking questions
103   Card reversals and reconcilers

107   PART 4: INTERPRETING THE CARDS

108   Look for patterns

109   Look for multiples

110   Look for connections

112   Look for symbols

113   Trust your intuition

115   Tarot spreads to try

132   Extra resources

133   PART 5: A MYSTIC LIFE

133   Find your power card

134   Bring love into your life

136   Couple goals

138   Mend a broken heart

143   Attract wealth

146   Contact your guardian angels

149   Interpret dreams

150   Discover your past life

152   Cleanse your chakras

154   Establish timing

157   END NOTE

157   Is the outcome fixed?

INTRODUCTION

The Tarot is a deck of 78 cards that are used for divination. In a reading, a number of cards are drawn from the pack at random and the unique symbolism of each card reveals the answer to any question you may wish to explore. No one knows for certain how the Tarot works. Some people believe the cards are guided by angels or spirits. Others believe that each reading is a perfect example of synchronicity, where the cards selected have no causal relationship yet seem to be meaningfully related.

Contrary to popular belief, anyone can read the Tarot. You don't need to be psychic or spend years training, as the images on the cards are powerful and universal. The best way to get started is to dive right in with a deck of cards that resonates with you personally (see p.86 for some advice on how to choose one).

This little book will guide you on your journey, introducing you to the cards one by one with simple descriptions to help you decode the symbolism and remember their meanings. There are sample spreads to follow and lots of different readings to try, focusing on everything from spirituality to romance to your career. It's time to step inside the world of the Tarot and begin your voyage to self-discovery. Enjoy!

PART 1

THE HISTORY OF TAROT

Strange though it may seem, the Tarot began life as a trick-taking card game known as Tarrocchi, Trionfi or Trumps, which is still played in parts of Europe today.

THE GAME OF TAROT

Card games were introduced to the parlours of Europe in the fourteenth century, using decks of playing cards with four suits – similar to the modern suits of hearts, spades, clubs and diamonds. (These suit cards eventually became the Cups, Pentacles, Swords and Wands of the Tarot's minor arcana.)

Only the nobility could afford these hand-painted cards. They personalized their decks, commissioning extra cards with allegorical scenes or family members. These were used in games as trump cards and the game of Tarot started to evolve. (These trump cards eventually became the Tarot's major arcana.)

The invention of the movable-type printing press in the fifteenth century meant that playing cards became accessible to more people, and the names of the cards became more standardized.

The Fool –
Tarot of Marseilles,
eighteenth century

The Fool – Smith-Rider-Waite, nineteenth century

TAROT FOR DIVINATION

Cartomancy, or card divination, has existed since the invention of playing cards. However, Tarot cards weren't used for divination until the eighteenth century – until then their purpose had been purely for games. It happened after occultist Antoine Court de Gébelin popularized the idea that Tarot cards were based on the secrets of the Ancient Egyptians, despite a lack of evidence.

During the nineteenth century, interest in the esoteric side of the Tarot boomed. The first deck to show individual scenes on the minor arcana (instead of patterns of Pentacles, Cups, Swords and Wands) was published. This deck, known as the Smith-Rider-Waite, is still popular today.

The cards in this book are designed by Jeffrey Thompson, using a woodcut style and drawing on the symbolism of the Smith-Rider-Waite.

The Fool - Jeffrey Thompson, modern

PART 2

THE CARDS

The Tarot deck is made up of 22 major arcana cards and 56 minor arcana cards.

MAJOR ARCANA

These cards are archetypes that represent the karmic influences and themes at work in your life. When one appears in a reading, you are being called to reflect on the life lessons it offers.

MINOR ARCANA

These cards are grouped into four suits. Each suit contains 14 cards, similar to those in a traditional deck of playing cards. There are ten numbered cards: Ace /1 (p.66), 2 (p.67), 3 (p.68), 4 (p.69), 5 (p.70), 6 (p.71), 7 (p.72), 8 (p.73), 9 (p.74), 10 (p.75); and four court cards: Page (p.82), Knight (p.83), Queen (p.84) and King (p.85).

These cards describe situations, help you make choices, reflect your state of mind and give you advice.

When a reading is mostly made up of major arcana, fate is in control and it is likely you are experiencing a lot of big changes. If the major arcana cards are reversed, it could be a sign that you are not paying enough attention to the bigger picture. If the reading is made up of mostly minor arcana, it is more concerned with the day to day.

CARD REVERSALS

In a spread, cards can be described as "upright" or "reversed". A card is "reversed" when it appears upside down.

Upright

Reversed

THE MAJOR ARCANA

QUICK REFERENCE GUIDE

0 The Fool – 0 (see p.16)
1 The Magician – I (see p.18)
2 The High Priestess – II (see p.20)
3 The Empress – III (see p.22)
4 The Emperor – IV (see p.24)
5 The Hierophant – V (see p.26)
6 The Lovers – VI (see p.28)
7 The Chariot – VII (see p.30)
8 Strength – VIII (see p.32)
9 The Hermit – IX (see p.34)
10 The Wheel of Fortune – X (see p.36)
11 Justice – XI (see p.38)
12 The Hanged Man – XII (see p.40)
13 Death – XIII (see p.42)
14 Temperance – XIV (see p.44)
15 The Devil – XV (see p.46)
16 The Tower – XVI (see p.48)
17 The Star – XVII (see p.50)
18 The Moon – XVIII (see p.52)
19 The Sun – XIX (see p.54)
20 Judgement – XX (see p.56)
21 The World – XXI (see p.58)

| The Fool | The Magician | The High Priestess | The Empress |

| The Emperor | The Hierophant | The Lovers | The Chariot |

| Strength | The Hermit | The Wheel of Fortune |

| Justice | The Hanged Man | Death | Temperance |

| The Devil | The Tower | The Star | The Moon |

| The Sun | Judgement | The World |

CARD 0: THE FOOL – 0

The sun shines as a young man sets off on his travels, wandering the world with a bag on his back, a flower in his hand and a dog at his heels. He is not looking at the path in front of him as he trusts life to steer him in the right direction – even as he steps over the edge of a cliff.

MEANINGS

- The Fool suggests the start of a journey, either actual or metaphorical. It can speak of the need to explore and the desire for adventure.

- Reversed, it can point to a lack of freedom, or someone who is childish and irresponsible. Remember – this could be someone you know or it could be you!

At a glance

Upright	Reversed
Innocence	Naivety
Spontaneity	Risk taking
Positive change	Negative change

***If the fool would persist in his
folly, he would become wise.***

William Blake

CARD 1: THE MAGICIAN – I

A robed man points one hand to the sky, to show where he draws his power from, and the other hand to the earth, where he manifests this power. Above his head, the sun blazes like a halo and we see a lemniscate, or infinity symbol. On a table are items that symbolize the suits of the minor arcana: a Pentacle, a Sword, a Cup and a Wand.

MEANINGS

- This card indicates the start of a new cycle in your life. This is a good time to start a new romance or enterprise. Embrace your inner power, pay attention to your inner voice and look out for a flash of inspiration.

- Reversed, this card warns of pride, egotism and misuse of power. It can suggest that someone is trying to trick you.

THE MAGICIAN

At a glance

Upright	**Reversed**
Power	Manipulation
Beginnings	Bad planning
Self-belief	Arrogance

As above, so below.

Hermes Trismegistus

CARD 2: THE HIGH PRIESTESS – II

A woman holds a sacred scroll and wears a sacred headdress. The moon is at her feet. She sits between two pillars, Jachin and Boaz, named after those at King Solomon's temple. This is the gateway to the Tarot and represents duality. (For example, negative/positive, dark/light.)

MEANINGS

- This is a card of mystery, wisdom and spiritual growth. It appears when you need to use intuition rather than logic to find an answer to your problems.

- Reversed, this card suggests painful secrets, gossip, or people talking behind your back. It can also hint at irrational behaviour and a lack of self-belief.

THE PRIESTESS

At a glance

Upright	Reversed
Wisdom	Superficiality
Intuition	Ignoring your intuition
Sacred mysteries	Harmful secrets

*All truths are easy to understand
once they are discovered; the
point is to discover them.*

Galileo Galilei

CARD 3: THE EMPRESS – III

A pregnant woman sits on a throne in a cornfield. Behind her a stream runs past a dark forest. She wears a crown and above it are 12 stars that represent the signs of the zodiac. Her authority is shown by the sceptre in her hand and the eagle shield at her feet.

MEANINGS

- This card is all about fertility, and can refer to a time when your mind is full of creative ideas, as well as – in a few cases – an actual pregnancy. If you want to paint, to write, to learn a new language, this card is your inspiration.

- Reversed, your creativity is being stifled and you need to spend more time in nature, or doing things that nourish your soul. In questions about a relationship, the reversed Empress can point to infidelity.

At a glance

Upright	Reversed
Mother figure	Co-dependence
Fertility	Infertility
Creativity	Creative block

There is no difficulty that enough love will not conquer.

Emmet Fox

CARD 4: THE EMPEROR – IV

A man sits on a throne high in the mountains. The eagle on his shield and the lion on his throne represent power and leadership. He rules with absolute authority and, although he is compassionate, will punish anyone who breaks his laws.

MEANINGS

- This card is a great reminder of how powerful it is to really want something. Other people may disagree with your goals, but if you fix your intention, you will move forwards.

- Reversed, it can suggest that you're being affected by someone who is weak and unambitious, or controlling and arrogant. Look at the surrounding cards to help you work out who that is – it could even be a part of yourself.

IV

I THE EMPEROR I

At a glance

Upright	Reversed
Structure	Inflexibility
Authority	Domination
Father figure	Controlling

Become a leader you can believe in.

Stan Slap

CARD 5: THE HIEROPHANT – V

A man in a priest's robes and hat stands in front of two pillars that support an arch. He holds a triple cross in one hand and blesses two monks with the other. At his feet is the key to all knowledge.

MEANINGS

- This card suggests a time to learn from other people's wisdom, follow established rules and stick to traditional values. Teachers come in all shapes and sizes, and yours could be a spiritual leader, tutor, family member or friend.

- Reversed, you find yourself clashing with an authority figure, or feeling confused about whom to trust.

THE *HIEROPHANT.

At a glance

Upright	Reversed
Determination	Stubbornness
Stability	Rigidity
Education	Conformity

*The thing you resist is the thing
you most need to hear.*

Robert Anthony

CARD 6: THE LOVERS - VI

A man and woman stand naked in a walled garden. An apple tree and snake hint at the biblical story of Adam and Eve in the Garden of Eden. In some decks, the angel Raphael appears beneath the sun. The O shape of the sun and M shape of the couple's arms spell "OM", a mantra with a high spiritual vibration.

MEANINGS

- This card can show harmony and attraction between lovers, but often indicates that there is an important choice to be made. (In the Bible story, Adam and Eve chose to eat the forbidden fruit and were thrown out of Paradise.)

- Reversed, the card can represent temptation in a relationship or warn that you are making choices that will have an unhappy outcome.

At a glance

Upright	Reversed
Love	Ego
Choices	Indecision
Duality	Inner conflict

Love is all about choices.

Kurt Smith

CARD 7: THE CHARIOT – VII

A man stands in a chariot, pulled by two lions, one black and one white. He holds a spear and a shield. He is calm and in control, and appears to be steering the chariot using the strength of his willpower alone. This can't be easy – especially if the lions want to go in two different directions.

MEANINGS

- The Chariot suggests a situation that requires personal strength. You will overcome any obstacles as long as you have faith in yourself; don't give up or try to take short cuts.

- Reversed, you may be suffering from a lack of focus and find yourself being pulled off course.

THE CHARIOT

At a glance

Upright	Reversed
Victory	Pyrrhic victory
Ambition	Conflict
Willpower	Setbacks

The hardest victory is over self.

Aristotle

CARD 8: STRENGTH – VIII

A woman gently strokes a lion she has tamed. Her face is calm and half in shadow. She wears flowers in her hair and flowers bloom at her feet despite the stars behind her showing it to be night-time. This is the card of fortitude: courage in the face of adversity.

MEANINGS

- When this card appears, you know you have a store of inner strength to draw on. You work from a position of love, which could lead others to underestimate your power.

- Reversed, you could be suffering from low self-esteem, aggressive behaviour or an inability to control your emotions.

At a glance

Upright	Reversed
Inner calm	Aggression
Head over heart	Heart over head
Confidence	Insecurity

With the new day comes new strength.

Eleanor Roosevelt

CARD 9: THE HERMIT - IX

An old man walks alone, high in the mountains, wearing a cloak that covers his face. It is night, and the landscape is stark and empty, but he has a staff to lean on and a lantern to show others the way.

MEANINGS

- This card suggests the need to take some time alone, where you can reflect on your life without distraction. Perhaps it is time to re-evaluate the path you are on? Perhaps you have learnt lessons that you can pass on to others? If so, this card is a helpful influence.

- Reversed, it could show that you have been on your own for too long, or are spending too much time in your own head and need to re-enter the world.

THE HERMIT

At a glance

Upright	Reversed
Soul-searching	Self-absorption
Solitude	Withdrawal
Inner guidance	Emptiness

In order to understand the world, one has to turn away from it on occasion.

Albert Camus

CARD 10: THE WHEEL OF FORTUNE - X

In the starry night sky, the karmic wheel spins, representing the endless cycle of death and rebirth. Inside it are the alchemical symbols for water, sulphur, salt and mercury. These are the building blocks of life. The lion is a reminder that the wheel is always turning. One day you are at the top, the next you are underneath it.

MEANINGS

- This card can refer to the passing of time, the promise of good luck and a warning not to let opportunities pass you by.

- Reversed, it can show that you are not in control of your life, or hint at karmic debts being paid.

WHEEL OF FORTUNE

At a glance

Upright	Reversed
Good luck	Bad luck
Destiny	No control
Karma	Breaking a cycle

How people treat you is their
karma; how you react is yours.

Wayne Dyer

CARD 11: JUSTICE - XI

A woman balances in the heavens, the stars and sun spread out behind her. In one hand she carries the sword of truth and, in the other, a set of scales to weigh up good deeds and bad ones. Her blindfold shows that she is an impartial judge.

MEANINGS

- This card advises you to take responsibility for your own actions, past and present. The decisions you are making now will have consequences, or past decisions are coming back to haunt you. Legal decisions will be settled happily, if you play fair.

- Reversed, it can refer to divorce, or unfair legal settlements. It can point to someone who would rather blame past events than take responsibility for their actions.

At a glance

Upright	**Reversed**
Fairness	Unfairness
Truth	Dishonesty
Law	Unaccountability

Win or lose, do it fairly.

Knute Rockne

CARD 12: THE HANGED MAN – XII

A man dangles upside-down from a tree. By rights, he should be furious, but he looks calm and there is a halo behind his head. From this position, he sees things the way they truly are, and when he comes down from the tree he will never see things in the same way again.

MEANINGS

- This is a card of deep psychic power and upside-down truths. At this time, you move forward by standing still. What is needed is rest and reflection rather than action. You may feel your life has been somehow suspended.

- Reversed, this card can describe someone who is selfish or impatient. Alternatively, it can refer to someone who is too giving or only sees things from one side.

At a glance

Upright	Reversed
Patience	Delay
Awakening	Indecision
Surrender	Restrictions

Surrender to what is. Let go of what was. Have faith in what will be.

Sonia Ricotti

CARD 13: DEATH – XIII

A skeleton riding on a pale horse kicks up the dust. This is a reminder of the words, "Ashes to ashes, dust to dust", often read at funerals. He carries a banner depicting three bright suns, but behind him the sun in the sky is black. The sun is a symbol of death and rebirth, dying daily at sunset and being reborn each morning at sunrise.

MEANINGS

- Although it can appear to refer to a recent brush with death, or the death of a loved one, this card is more likely to be about change, or the death of a comfortable mode of being.

- Reversed, it suggests a refusal to change and warns of the pitfalls of stagnation.

At a glance

Upright	Reversed
Transition	Stagnation
Change	Resistance
Release	Limbo

Inner peace is shaped by the wisdom that "this too shall pass".

Tania Ahsan

CARD 14: TEMPERANCE – XIV

This card is all about balancing opposing forces. An angel, who is both male and female, stands with one foot on the ground and the other in the water, pouring water between two vessels. The white sun, black water and white earth hint at the elements of the yin/yang symbol.

MEANINGS

- This card is concerned with moderation, avoiding extremes and taking a middle path. Under its influence, you can blend things together that previously seemed irreconcilable to create something new. This could be feelings, people or events – you will know what needs to be combined and modified.

- Reversed, the card suggests that something in your life is out of balance, causing anxiety and stress.

At a glance

Upright	Reversed
Balance	Imbalance
Moderation	Excess
Purpose	Stress

Success is balance.
Laila Ali

CARD 15: THE DEVIL – XV

A devil with horns and wings holds a naked man and woman in chains. An inverted pentagram symbolizes the prioritization of earthly matters over spiritual. The chains these people wear are loose, suggesting they could slip out of them – if only they wanted to.

MEANINGS

- This is the card of addictions or addictive behaviour. It can suggest you are trapped by certain desires or thoughts, and that you are refusing to take responsibility for making changes.

- Reversed, this card can point to a refusal to change or an inability to see the positive side of life.

At a glance

Upright	Reversed
Challenge	Manipulation
Desire	Addiction
Ambition	Obsession

The devil doesn't come dressed in a red cape and pointy horns. He comes as everything you've ever wished for.

Tucker Max

CARD 16: THE TOWER – XVI

A tower has been hit by a sudden bolt of lightning. Flames shoot out of the windows and people fall to the ground as it crumbles. The sky is dark, but the light on the horizon suggests that the sun is about to rise, hinting at the old saying: "The darkest hour is just before dawn."

MEANINGS

- It is important to pay attention when the Tower appears in a reading. This card suggests unexpected change or a sudden shock that knocks you sideways. It's a reminder that you can't control the things life throws at you, but you can control your reactions. Life-changing events can lead to better opportunities.

- Reversed, this card shows a fear of change, or a major crisis averted.

At a glance

Upright	Reversed
Upheaval	Fear of change
Unexpected events	Reversal of fortune
Crisis	Revelation

There is nothing permanent except change.

Heraclitus

CARD 17: THE STAR - XVII

A man looks through his telescope at a huge star in the sky. Seven other stars form a gentle curve above him. In many decks, such as the Smith-Rider-Waite, this card shows a naked woman kneeling by a pool, pouring water into the pool and on to the land.

MEANINGS

- This card suggests that you have been through a challenging time, but things are getting better. You have survived and gained insights that you didn't have before. This is a restful card, and it brings with it the hope of healing and the advice to trust in the universe.

- Reversed, the card can suggest someone who is running away from their problems, self-doubt and negativity.

At a glance

Upright	Reversed
Confidence	Negativity
Hope	Avoidance
Respite	Lack of help

The cosmos is within us.
We are made of star stuff.

Carl Sagan

CARD 18: THE MOON - XVIII

A moonlit path leads between two pillars, where a dog and a wolf represent the tame and the wild aspects of nature. The moon has a dark side as well as a light one. A lobster crawls out of the water, representing the unconscious mind.

MEANINGS

- This is a card of psychic development and connects deeply to your subconscious mind. It can warn you of hidden danger, advise you to look carefully at the road ahead, or suggest that you are finding it hard to tell the difference between real and imagined concerns.

- Reversed, this card can warn of bad luck, or suggest that problems that seem real are in your head.

At a glance

Upright	Reversed
Illusion	Distress
Subconscious	Repression
Intuition	Anxiety

*The moon is the first milestone
on the road to the stars.*

Arthur C. Clarke

CARD 19: THE SUN – XIX

The sun beats down enthusiastically on rows of sunflowers growing tall in a walled garden. Sunflowers symbolize loyalty and in Christianity are a sign of God's love. Some decks show children on this card, which highlights the childlike innocence of the card's joyful message.

MEANINGS

- This is an optimistic card and it offers a positive outcome to your questions. When it appears in your reading, expect a time of confidence and success, and any negative feelings will quickly pass. Expect good health, happiness and abundance.

- Reversed, this card can suggest an absence of joy, and is a reminder to allow more love and laughter into your life.

At a glance

Upright	Reversed
Positivity	Negativity
Warmth	Lack of love
Success	Repressed inner child

When the sun is shining
I can do anything.
Wilma Rudolph

CARD 20: JUDGEMENT - XX

An angel in a cloud blows a trumpet and the dead rise joyfully from their graves. This scene refers to the day of judgement in the Bible - the time at the end of the world when the dead awake, their sins are forgiven, and they move on to live in heaven.

MEANINGS

- This powerful card is all about processing old memories, forgiving yourself for past mistakes and judging without condemnation. This is a time to take stock, to see how you got to where you are now.

- Reversed, it refers to a refusal to learn from past mistakes, a harsh judgement or an inability to love yourself.

At a glance

Upright	Reversed
Processing	Delays
Salvation	Guilt
Forgiving	Obstinacy

Be courageous enough to forgive
yourself; never forget to be
compassionate to yourself.

Debasish Mridha

CARD 21: THE WORLD – XXI

A woman holding two batons dances beyond the Earth, surrounded by the ouroboros – a snake eating its tail in a symbol of eternity. She represents a human soul that has reached the end of its spiritual journey and become one with the world. An eagle, lion, man and bull in the corners of the card symbolize the harmony between the energies of the four fixed signs of the zodiac: Scorpio, Leo, Aquarius and Taurus.

MEANINGS

- As the final card of the major arcana, the World represents fulfilment and achievement. You have accomplished something great or completed a project.

- Reversed, it can suggest that something is missing from your life, a feeling of disconnection and a lack of closure.

At a glance

Upright	Reversed
Freedom	Depression
Completion	Stagnation
Achievement	Emptiness

***Everything turns in circles and spirals
with the cosmic heart until infinity.***

Suzy Kassem

THE FOOL'S JOURNEY

The Fool's Journey is a metaphor for the journey through life. It is a story that has been passed down by Tarot readers over the years, to help you remember the meanings of the cards and deepen your understanding of them. In the story, the Fool we meet in Card 0 sets out on his travels and meets each of the cards of the major arcana in turn, learning a different life lesson with each one.

0   **The Fool** – the Fool is about to step off the edge of a cliff. Is this the end? He closes his eyes and his life flashes before him...

1   **The Magician** – like many good heroes, the Fool has two sets of parents. This is his spiritual father.

2   **High Priestess** – and his spiritual mother.

3   **The Empress** – this is his earthly mother.

4   **The Emperor** – and his earthly father.

5   **The Hierophant** – the Fool has much to learn. He goes to school and is taught the rules of society.

6   **The Lovers** – he meets a woman and learns about love.

7 The Chariot – the Fool is growing up and must deal with the challenges of the earthly world. He leaves home and sets out on his own, starting to make choices for himself.

8 Strength – worldly experiences strengthen his inner wisdom.

9 The Hermit – he finds a guide to help him discover the deeper meaning of life.

10 The Wheel of Fortune – the Fool learns about karma and the cycles of life.

11 Justice – he learns about duality and the need for balance.

12 The Hanged Man – the Fool has a spiritual awakening and gains a different perspective on life. He is ready to take on the challenges of the spiritual world.

13 Death – the Fool is reborn.

14 Temperance – he meets an angel who teaches him to balance the opposing forces within him.

15 The Devil – he is tempted by a devil who challenges him to truly see himself.

16 The Tower – he reaches a tower he remembers building in his youth and watches as it is destroyed by lightning. He feels lost and unable to go on.

17 Star – he rests and is comforted by a magical being called Hope.

18 The Moon – the moon rises and the Fool sees the path ahead. It is familiar; one that he glimpsed as a child.

19 The Sun – the path leads him to a garden full of sunflowers, where he is greeted by a small boy. He recognizes his own inner child and feels truly happy for the first time.

20 Judgement – a fiery angel summons up the spectres of the Fool's past selves. He meets them with compassion, forgives them and they vanish.

21 The World – the Fool opens his eyes and sees that he is still on the edge of the cliff. He steps over the edge but doesn't fall. Instead he finds himself dancing in the sky, at one with the universe.

In time, the characters of the major arcana will become familiar friends. You might even catch yourself saying, "What a High Priestess kind of day" or "This is a bit of a Hanged Man situation". But now, we need to move on and meet the more "day-to-day" cards of the minor arcana.

THE MINOR ARCANA

Each of the four suits of the minor arcana has a set of associations, as follows:

Cups
Represent: relationships, emotions and desires
Element: water
Icon: golden chalice

Swords
Represent: thoughts, ideas and conflict
Element: air
Icon: sword

Pentacles
Represent: possessions, money and career
Element: earth
Icon: coin with the pattern of a five-pointed star

Wands
Represent: energy, spirituality and growth
Element: fire
Icon: a wooden stick or rod

NUMBERS

If remembering the meanings of all the cards seems daunting, start by learning the keywords for each number, as follows:

- Aces are about beginnings
- Twos are about balance
- Threes are about growth
- Fours are about stability
- Fives are about challenge
- Sixes are about triumphs
- Sevens are about choices
- Eights are about movement
- Nines are about attainment
- Tens are about completion

Then, using your knowledge of the four suits, you can work out what a card is about.

For example:

Ace of Cups

Aces are about beginnings.

Cups are about emotions.

So, the Ace of Cups could point to a new relationship.

Six of Pentacles

Sixes are about triumphs.

Pentacles are about money and career.

So, the Six of Pentacles could describe a promotion at work.

If you like memory rhymes, this can help you remember the keywords.

1, 2, 3 – B, B, G.

4, 5, 6 – S, C, T.

7, 8 is C and M.

A and C is 9 and 10.

ACES

Ace of Cups
Your cup overflows
Upright: love, optimism, fresh start
Reversed: emotional instability, stagnation, ego

Ace of Swords
The sword of truth
Upright: mental clarity, new ideas, time for change
Reversed: painful truths, fear of new ideas

Ace of Wands
A burst of energy
Upright: energy, adventure, confidence
Reversed: cancelled plans, stagnation, depression

Ace of Pentacles
Material matters
Upright: achievement, prosperity, financial luck
Reversed: greed, jealousy, financial disappointment

TWOS

Two of Cups
A loving balance
Upright: harmony, balance, good fortune
Reversed: misunderstandings, incompatibility, divorce

Two of Swords
At a crossroads
Upright: tension, an uneasy truce, unclear future
Reversed: lack of responsibility, putting off a decision

Two of Wands
Eyes on the horizon
Upright: future success, delays, making plans
Reversed: impatience, bad planning

Two of Pentacles
Juggling life
Upright: adaptability, versatility, extra workload
Reversed: financial problems, depression, coping issues

THREES

Three of Cups
A celebration of friendship
Upright: family, holidays, celebrations
Reversed: gossip, overindulgence, false friends

Three of Swords
Heartbreak
Upright: betrayal, ill health, separation
Reversed: confusion, pain, disconnection

Three of Wands
The brink of success
Upright: inspiration, enthusiasm, marriage
Reversed: carelessness, inability to take charge

Three of Pentacles
Practice makes perfect
Upright: qualifications, talent, expertise
Reversed: overqualified, under-skilled, self-doubt

FOURS

Four of Cups
Don't ignore opportunities
Upright: uncertainty, boredom, frustration
Reversed: fear of commitment, unrealistic expectations

Four of Swords
Retreating from life
Upright: withdrawal, convalescence, imprisonment
Reversed: doing too much, burnt out

Four of Wands
Celebrate your achievements
Upright: stability, success, moving to the next stage
Reversed: family tensions, period of transition

Four of Pentacles
Money on the mind
Upright: security, avarice, clinging to possessions
Reversed: too much spending or too much saving

FIVES

Five of Cups
Memories in the way
Upright: disappointment, self-pity, regret
Reversed: separation, trust issues, fear of the future

Five of Swords
Hollow victory
Upright: infidelity, unfair battles, unhealthy mental attitudes
Reversed: lack of compromise, discord, destruction

Five of Wands
Rise to the challenge
Upright: competition, rivalry, need for flexibility
Reversed: petty fighting, power struggles, selfishness

Five of Pentacles
Crisis point
Upright: illness, unemployment, need for guidance
Reversed: refusal to look for help, lack of hope

SIXES

Six of Cups
A connection to the past
Upright: memories, past efforts rewarded, old friends
Reversed: nostalgia, outdated feelings or relationships

Six of Swords
Moving to higher ground
Upright: withdrawal, distance, travel
Reversed: delayed plans, need for escape

Six of Wands
Victory
Upright: recognition, advancement, success
Reversed: pride, egotism, success for others

Six of Pentacles
Giving and receiving
Upright: charity, generosity, synchronicities
Reversed: selfishness, unwanted gifts, misfortune

SEVENS

Seven of Cups
Too many choices
Upright: false choices, indecision, lack of focus
Reversed: living in a fantasy world, lack of self-belief

Seven of Swords
Be on your guard
Upright: trickery, suspicions, quarrels
Reversed: guilt, jealousy, lack of trust

Seven of Wands
Stand your ground
Upright: lots of small problems, perseverance
Reversed: distractions, giving up, overwhelmed

Seven of Pentacles
Take a step back
Upright: evaluation, effort, hard work
Reversed: frustration, anxiety, poor planning

EIGHTS

Eight of Cups

Leaving the past behind

Upright: new purpose, changing attitudes, moving on

Reversed: separation, anxiety, outgrowing a relationship

Eight of Swords

Unable to walk away

Upright: trapped, hopeless, lack of information

Reversed: cycle of negativity, lack of confidence

Eight of Wands

Life speeding up

Upright: travel, excitement, opportunities

Reversed: need to slow down, getting left behind

Eight of Pentacles

Getting things done

Upright: new skills, learning, responsibility

Reversed: laziness, dishonesty, refusal to learn

NINES

Nine of Cups
In tune with the world
Upright: luck, contentment, success
Reversed: laziness, indulgence, excess

Nine of Swords
Sleepless nights
Upright: nightmares, anxiety, depression
Reversed: crisis point, start of recovery

Nine of Wands
Been through the wars
Upright: need for resilience, one last challenge
Reversed: lack of preparation, exhaustion

Nine of Pentacles
A time of prosperity
Upright: financial stability, material comfort, solitude
Reversed: bad investments, loneliness, theft

TENS

Ten of Cups
Happy families
Upright: home, family, harmony
Reversed: betrayal, loss, parenting problems

Ten of Swords
The end of a negative cycle
Upright: relief, change, hard-earned wisdom
Reversed: betrayal, melodrama, forced changes

Ten of Wands
Taking on responsibility
Upright: duty, heavy burdens, refusal to delegate
Reversed: unkindness, lack of responsibility

Ten of Pentacles
Material security
Upright: investment, confidence, prosperity
Reversed: financial burdens, family debt

This exercise is designed to help you get to know the suits of the minor arcana:

1. Shuffle the whole deck, silently stating that your intention is to use the minor arcana to get a snapshot of what's on your mind in the present moment.

2. Cut the deck into three piles with your dominant hand (this is your right if you are right-handed and left if you are left-handed).

3. Restack the cards, then turn the first card over and place it at the side of the deck, face up.

4. Continue turning over the cards one by one until you have one card from each of the four suits, Pentacles, Wands, Swords and Cups, in front of you.

5. Now look at the order in which the suits appear and note their associations. The order will show you what's on your mind at the moment – from most to least important. To recap:

- Swords – you're full of ideas – or worries! Either way, you are spending a lot of time in your head.

- Wands – you have plans you want to put in motion, places you want to go, people to see.

- Cups – you are thinking about love, relationships, past, present and future.

- Pentacles – you are thinking about money – how to get it, what to do with it.

Swords   Wands

Cups   Pentacles

THE COURT CARDS

Each suit of the minor arcana contains a Page, Knight, Queen and King. They are the 16 "people cards" and there are a number of ways to interpret them.

A court card can refer to:

Your personality

What are you bringing to the situation?

How are you responding to the situation?

The personality of someone you know

Is this card referring to a real person you know, such as a parent, boss or friend?

How are they influencing the situation?

The personality of the situation

What energy is affecting the situation?

What energy is needed in this situation?

If remembering the meanings of all the cards seems daunting, start by learning the symbolism of each rank, as follows:

Rank	Age	Energy
Page	Child	Beginning
Knight	Youth	Moving
Queen	Mature feminine	Nurturing
King	Mature masculine	Accomplishing

Remember:

- Masculine and feminine energies can apply to women or men.

- Try not to think of any of these energies as "better" than another. They all have important parts to play, just like the stages of a successful project:

  1. Have an idea for a project (Page energy)

  2. Start the project (Knight energy)

  3. See the project through (Queen energy)

  4. Complete the project (King energy)

- Once you are familiar with this idea, you can use your knowledge of the four suits to work out what a card is about.

For example:

Page of Pentacles

Pages are about beginnings.

Pentacles are about money and career.

So, the Page of Pentacles could bring a message about a new job.

The most important question to ask when a court card appears in a reading is: "How is this kind of personality shaping events?" Which is why it is worth getting to know the cards as people.

This exercise is designed to help you think about the different personalities of the court cards in a personal way. It will help you commit them to memory.

1. Take the 16 court cards out of the deck and deal them into a row.

2. Imagine these have created a scene from a tapestry or painting.

3. Look at the way the characters are interacting with each other, asking yourself questions like:

    *   "Is that Knight galloping towards or away from that King?"

    *   "Is that Queen looking sadly or angrily at that Page?"

    *   "Who is that Page staring at?"

    *   "Who do these people remind me of?"

4. Compare your ideas with the keywords on the next five pages.

5. Now move the order of the cards around and watch the relationships shift. How has the story changed?

PAGES

Pages can represent a message, an opportunity, starting something new, a new person in your life.

Page of Cups
Archetype: the dreamer
Upright: trusting
Reversed: vulnerable

Page of Swords
Archetype: the observer
Upright: truthful
Reversed: detached

Page of Wands
Archetype: the explorer
Upright: adventurous
Reversed: directionless

Page of Pentacles
Archetype: the student
Upright: enthusiastic
Reversed: lazy

KNIGHTS

Knights can represent an invitation, a quest, getting things moving, boundless energy.

Knight of Cups
Archetype: the faithful lover
Upright: charming
Reversed: self-absorbed

Knight of Swords
Archetype: the fighter
Upright: combative
Reversed: closed-minded

Knight of Wands
Archetype: the action hero
Upright: impulsive
Reversed: hasty

Knight of Pentacles
Archetype: the practical friend
Upright: reliable
Reversed: cautious

QUEENS

Queens can represent emotional strength, problem-solving, wisdom, leadership.

Queen of Cups
Archetype: the family figure
Upright: accepting
Reversed: controlling

Queen of Swords
Archetype: the unconventional
Upright: clear thinking
Reversed: cruel

Queen of Wands
Archetype: the socializer
Upright: assertive
Reversed: bossy

Queen of Pentacles
Archetype: the business executive
Upright: confident
Reversed: superficial

KINGS

Kings can represent power and authority, expertise, decision-making, success.

King of Cups
Archetype: the provider
Upright: loyal
Reversed: untrustworthy

King of Swords
Archetype: the intellectual
Upright: challenging
Reversed: unkind

King of Wands
Archetype: the entrepreneur
Upright: ambitious
Reversed: overbearing

King of Pentacles
Archetype: the businessman
Upright: responsible
Reversed: impractical

PART 3

USING THE CARDS

Now that you've learnt the basic meanings of both the major and minor arcana, let's look at how you can use them in your Tarot readings.

CHOOSING A DECK

There's an old superstition about it being bad luck to buy your own Tarot cards and that it's better to be gifted your first deck. However, if you are keen to start learning, there is really no reason why you shouldn't pick out your own cards. If you don't, you could end up waiting a really long time or end up with a deck that doesn't really suit you.

Do some research and choose a deck that really speaks to you. It's important to have a good relationship with your cards, as if you find the imagery off-putting your readings aren't going to be very successful. "New Age" shops always have a great variety, but you could also look in a regular bookshop or online. There are lots of websites with pictures and reviews of the different packs on offer.

Make sure you buy a standard deck of Tarot cards, not a pack of oracle cards or one that contains only the major arcana. Although it is possible to do readings using just the trump cards, you won't be getting the full benefit.

If you don't know which deck to choose, the Smith-Rider-Waite is popular for good reason. The cards are detailed and easy to read, and the images are the pattern for countless other modern decks.

ENERGIZING YOUR NEW CARDS

Before you use a new deck, you need to give it a proper shuffle to energize the cards. Put the deck on a flat surface, fan it out, then give the cards a good swirl around in different directions until they are mixed up. When you gather them up again, the cards will be in a random order and some should be upside down, which will give reversals in your readings.

CLEANSING YOUR CARDS

Many readers will give their cards an energy cleanse if the deck hasn't been used for a long time, or to clear out any negative energy that has been stuck in the cards after a challenging reading.

Try one of these cleansing rituals:

- Shuffle the deck, then knock sharply on it three times, visualizing the stuck energy flying away.

- Give the cards a "moon bath" by placing them on a window ledge overnight, on the night of a full moon.

- Burn dried sage, or a smudge stick, and pass the cards through the smoke several times to cleanse the energy.

GETTING TO KNOW THE CARDS

It is a good idea to familiarize yourself with the cards in your deck before you start to do readings. Set aside an hour to immerse yourself in the imagery, one card at a time. A great way to do this is to imagine yourself as part of the picture on a card. If you're finding this a little tricky, try the following steps:

1. Pick a card and describe it out loud in as much detail as possible. Start with the physical aspects of the image, such as clothes and landscape, then move on to how you think the characters may be feeling and what they are doing, for example: "This is the Fool. A man wearing a short robe is stepping off the edge of a cliff. Behind him, a dog is barking. His eyes are firmly looking ahead..."

2. Now, repeat the description from your own point of view, for example: "I am the Fool. I am wearing a short robe as I step off the edge of a cliff. Behind me, a dog is barking. My eyes are firmly looking ahead..."

3. Take time to notice any pictures or words that come into your head and trust their value. When

you are describing the cards from your own point of view, do you find some parts of the picture easier to describe and some parts harder? Ask yourself why.

4. Return the card to the deck. Close your eyes, and breathe deeply in and out three times to bring your mind back to your body.

Try to involve the Tarot in your life on a daily basis, until it has become a routine. You could draw one card every morning and keep its message in your mind as you face the challenges of the day. Or, you could draw one card before you go to bed each night, study it and sleep with it under your pillow. Keep a notebook by your bed to record any interesting connections in your dreams.

SETTING THE SCENE

Of course, it's possible to do a tarot reading anywhere – at home, in the park, in a coffee shop – but while you are learning, it helps to find somewhere you feel relaxed and where you won't be disturbed.

You could set up a sacred space, using crystals, candles, flowers and incense arranged on and around a reading cloth. This place should have a positive energy, and be calm and free from other clutter. Light the candle to symbolize the start of the reading, then blow it out to symbolize the end.

Choose from these items to help you create your sacred space:

Candles
White candle – purity of intention
Purple candle – psychic ability

Crystals
Amethyst – spiritual protection
Clear quartz – positive energy

Incense
Cinnamon incense – protection and power
Sandalwood incense – spiritual awareness

Flowers
Daisy – positivity
Lavender – healing

Reading cloth
Purple – wisdom
Silver – intuition

If you prefer a pared-down setting, it's still a good idea
to use a reading cloth on which to deal your cards
when you lay out your spreads. This should be a piece
of material that you don't use for anything else and it
should be big enough to wrap the cards in when you're
not using them.

SETTING YOUR INTENTION

It's important to keep a positive flow of energy around yourself during a reading. One quick and easy way to purify a space and keep any negative energy at bay is to bathe the room in white light.

Try this:

- Start by visualizing a ball of bright, white light, in front of you at the level of your heart.

- Breathe deeply and picture it expanding to fill the room.

- As you imagine it reaching and cleansing every corner of the room, close your eyes and gently state the purity of your intention. For example: "I cleanse this room with beautiful white light. My intentions are pure."

- You are now ready to start your reading.

READING THE CARDS

If you are new to reading the cards, it's a good idea to start by practising with a basic three-card spread, such as "Past Present Future". This is also a great spread to use when you are more confident but need a quick reading.

Try this:
- Shuffle the deck and concentrate on your question.
- If any cards fly out of the deck while you shuffle – as if demanding to be noticed – then notice them! They are often symbolic.
- Deal three cards from the top of the deck, face up, in front of you. If you have shuffled the pack well, some of the cards could be reversed (upside down).

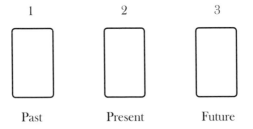

| 1 | 2 | 3 |
| Past | Present | Future |

Use the meanings in Part 2 to help you with these first three steps.

- Start by looking at the centre card, which describes your present situation.

- Then, move to the card on the left, which highlights any recent events that are having an effect on the situation.

- Finally, read the card on the right, which predicts how the situation will change in the near future, if things carry on as they are.

- Now you've seen what each card means separately, think about how the meanings flow together, as if they are combining to tell a story with a beginning, middle and end. If you find this tricky, there are plenty of tips in Part 4.

SAMPLE READING

Tilly's question

"I've been with my partner for three months and we are keen to move things to the next level. Things are going really well between us, but it feels like a really big step. Should we buy a flat together?"

Tilly's reading

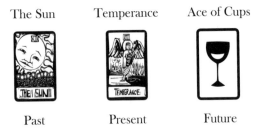

The Sun	Temperance	Ace of Cups
Past	Present	Future

Card by card

PRESENT: Patience is a keyword for the Temperance card (p.44).

PAST: The Sun (p.54) is a positive card that suggests a sense of vitality.

FUTURE: The Ace of Cups (p.66) shows that love is at the heart of the situation.

Note: The order in which the cards are dealt and read is different. The cards should be dealt in this order **past**, **present**, **future**, but read **present**, **past**, **future**.

Overall reading

Tilly and her partner share a sunny outlook on life. They probably have a lot of fun together, but is this enough to survive the leap into the real world of mortgages and broken boilers? Perhaps the couple need to wait a while before they make a decision. Patience has its rewards and the future looks bright, so it will be worth the wait.

TIPS FOR ASKING QUESTIONS

The more detailed the question you ask at the start of a reading, the more detailed your answer will be. Your question shouldn't include wishful thinking or false assumptions.

For example:

"Will I get promoted?" is vague.

"When will I get promoted?" is wishful thinking. (The answer could be "never".)

"Will I get promoted at work in the next six months?" is more specific, but it is not much of a conversation starter and the answer could still be a simple "no".

"What can I do to get a promotion at work in the next six months?" is a much better question. It opens up a conversation, allowing the cards to advise you on how to help yourself achieve your goals.

Another thing to remember is to always put yourself at the centre of the reading.

For example:

"Is my friend making the wrong decision?" places the focus on them.

"How can I help my friend make the right decision?" places the focus on you.

(Of course, if you are reading for a friend, it is fine for them to ask: "Am I making the wrong decision?")

Try to keep a clear mind when asking a question and focus on what you want to know. You have to believe that the cards can give you an answer, otherwise there is no point in asking. Tarot works best if you are willing to listen.

A note on reading for others

When you are reading the cards for someone else, be gentle with them. Remember that you are in a position of trust. Shaking your head at the sight of the Tower (p.48) and muttering, "Ooh, that's not good," when the Three of Swords (p.68) turns up, are not great ways to put someone at their ease. And if Death (p.42) puts in an appearance, make sure you address it before you start the reading. It is possible that the other person has had a recent traumatic experience you should know about. Even if this is not the case, it's not a bad idea to reassure them that the card is usually symbolic.

Keep in mind that it is *not* cheating to ask questions during a reading. If the other person is genuinely interested in what the cards have to say, they will be prepared to enter into a dialogue, happily let you know when things ring true and give some background on their situation. A cold reading, where you are being tested to see if the cards "get things right", is not going to be very satisfying for anyone involved.

SAMPLE READING

Cara's question

"I recently started a new job. It's hard and I miss my old colleagues. Have I made the right choice?"

Cara's reading

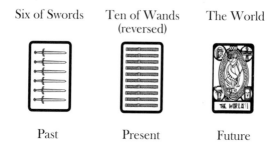

Six of Swords	Ten of Wands (reversed)	The World
Past	Present	Future

Card by card

PRESENT: Upright, the Ten of Wands refers to someone with a heavy burden. Reversed, this person is refusing to put that burden down.

PAST: The Six of Swords is about leaving things behind in order to move forward.

FUTURE: The World describes reaching the end of a cycle.

Note: The order in which the cards are dealt and read is different. The cards should be dealt in this order **past**, **present**, **future**, but read **present**, **past**, **future**.

Overall reading

Cara probably didn't find it easy to leave her old job. However, no matter how sad she is feeling, she is moving on to better things. New jobs bring new responsibilities, but has she taken on more than she needs to? Perhaps there are some responsibilities she can offload. Change is tough, but Cara can be sure that she is going in the right direction.

CARD REVERSALS
AND RECONCILERS

CARD REVERSALS

Don't panic if a few upside-down cards appear in your reading. Card reversals give the cards an extra layer of meaning and just by taking them into account you have doubled the possibilities of the deck.

It is important to remember that reversed cards do not always mean the opposite of their upright meaning. Although this is sometimes the case, they often appear to show that the energies of the upright card are being blocked. Perhaps you are not able to deal with the card's energies at the present time, or you have to work through a few things before you can move on?

You will need to look at the surrounding cards for hints as to how this reversal fits into this specific reading and trust your intuition to tell you what is going on.

RECONCILERS

If you want to find out how to deal with the blockages suggested by a card reversal, you can deal another card on top of it, called a reconciler.

For example:
- You draw the reversed Six of Pentacles.

- Upright, this would represent balance in financial matters. Reversed, it suggests you are giving out more money than you are getting.

- You deal a reconciler on top of it.

- This is the Empress, a card of strength and creativity, suggesting that these are the aspects you can draw on to get through this challenging time.

SAMPLE READING

Paul's question

"I really dread Monday mornings. My career is going nowhere, but I don't want to lose my regular income. Should I stay in my job?"

Paul's reading

King of Pentacles   Temperance   Three of Wands
(reversed)   (reversed)

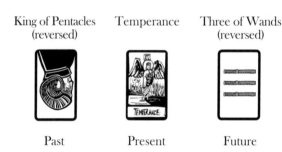

Past   Present   Future

Card by card

PRESENT: Temperance is a card of balance, patience and moderation.

PAST: The Reversed King of Pentacles can show someone stuck in a rut.

FUTURE: The Reversed Three of Wands suggests a lack of movement.

Note: The order in which the cards are dealt and read is different. The cards should be dealt in this order **past, present, future**, but read **present, past, future**.

Overall reading

Although status and finances are important to Paul, it seems likely that he is not exactly giving one hundred per cent at work. He needs to take time to realign himself with his purpose and think about what he really wants from his career. If the situation carries on as it is, there is nothing ahead but frustration.

PART 4

INTERPRETING THE CARDS

You've learnt about the cards and their associations, but you know that there's more to reading the Tarot than just looking up meanings in a book. So, what do you do next?

As with most skills in life, practice makes perfect. In order to tune in to your inner wisdom, you need to keep listening out for it – and a great way to do this is by making personal connections with your cards.

Reading the Tarot is not about memorizing a set of keywords. The cards are subtle, and their meanings shift according to the question being asked and their relation to the other cards in the spread. Start with the keywords for each card, but remember these are only prompts. They exist to kickstart your intuition into action. With the Tarot, you are always learning, no matter how long you have been reading the cards.

LOOK FOR PATTERNS

After you've examined the cards in a reading one by one, go back and look at the spread as a whole. Search for patterns and find the story. Ask yourself:

Do cards appear from all four suits?

A Tarot deck is a complete entity and the cards it chooses to hide can be revealing. Missing suits can suggest something is missing from your life. Remember that each suit has its own energies.

Are there more majors or minors?

A large number of majors can suggest that fate is playing a major role. The reading is dealing with things that have long-term consequences and are unavoidable. If the cards are mostly minors, the spread is looking at events that are of more short-term significance. More importantly, it suggests that things are in your hands. It's no use waiting for a life-changing event – you have to make some choices.

Are there linking themes?

If several cards have similar meanings, it can reinforce a certain idea or interpretation. Does it feel like some of the cards are "talking" to each other? Conversely, they may offer very different opinions on a situation. Look at the position they fall within the spread to get a clearer view.

LOOK FOR MULTIPLES

Have you dealt more than one card with the same number or several cards from the same suit? This could be meaningful within the context of your question or situation.

For example:

- Multiple Aces reinforce the idea that there are a lot of new things entering your life.

- Multiple Cups mean that love is an important issue.

- Multiple court cards mean that there are a lot of strong personalities at work.

Sometimes you find that you are getting the same card again and again, in different readings. This is a sign to pay attention. Perhaps you are ignoring the advice this card is giving. Or perhaps you keep asking the same question, despite the cards giving a clear answer.

If you really don't know why this particular card is so determined to make itself known, try dealing a reconciler on top of it (as described on p.104 for use with tricky reversals) to help you make sense of its message.

LOOK FOR CONNECTIONS

The more you get to know the cards in your deck, the more correspondences you will see between some of the cards. Some of the major arcana fall into natural pairs – such as the Emperor (p.24) and the Empress (p.22) – and some have more subtle connections.

For example:

- The High Priestess (p.20) and the Hierophant (p.26) are both placed between two pillars. Both cards are concerned with wisdom, but the High Priestess tells you to look inside for answers, while the Hierophant offers to teach them to you.

- The Chariot (p.30) and Strength (p.32) both feature lions. But the Chariot is all about outer power and Strength is about inner power.

- The Lovers (p.28) and the Devil (p.46) both depict naked couples, but one pair looks up at the sky and the other down at the ground. Both cards are about choices – ones to make or ones that have been made.

If there are obvious pairs in a reading, it is a good idea to look at them together. Perhaps one is in a "past" position and another in a "future"? Perhaps the cards are showing the difference between what you have been doing and what you need to do? Perhaps one shows you how you see yourself and the other how your friends see you?

Ask yourself where they fall in the spread, as it is their position and the other cards around them that will give you a clue to their deeper meaning.

LOOK FOR SYMBOLS

Have a look at what is going on in the background of
each card. Is it day or night? Sunny or cloudy? What
is in the distance – a hill to climb, a tower to reach, an
archway to go through? What do these symbols mean?
Nothing is there by accident!

For example:

- Flowers – growth
- Arches – new openings
- Paths – direction
- Pillars – balance
- Stars – inspiration
- Fish – intuition
- Birds – freedom
- Clouds – ideas
- Scrolls – knowledge
- Suns – expansion
- Moons – time
- Angels – guidance
- Castles – goals
- Horses – action
- Lions – courage
- Mountains – challenge

TRUST YOUR INTUITION

Call it a hunch, an instinct, a gut feeling – everyone has a sense of intuition, but trusting it can be hard.

There are many reasons to block this inner voice, such as overthinking, expecting too much or a fear of getting it wrong. Sometimes, the desire for something to be true is so strong that you can't even begin to entertain any other possibility.

The best way to get around all of these mental blocks is to find a quiet place and practice "tuning in" to your intuition.

This exercise uses the cards to help you listen to your inner voice:

- Pick a card at random and stare at the picture. Don't worry about trying to interpret what the picture is or means, just listen to your body. Does it make you feel happy? Anxious? Calm? Notice any associations, words, patterns, people, times or places that come up.

- Now, make a list of everything you see, from the number of birds in the sky to the length of the character's hair. You will be amazed at how many things you find to write about as you connect to the card.

- Finally, try to make up a story about what is going on in the picture. What are the people doing and why? Remind yourself that no idea is wrong when you are doing this exercise and let your intuition guide you.

Once you find that you are becoming more confident in your readings, you will probably want to explore different ways of laying out the cards to deal with specific areas or questions.

TAROT SPREADS TO TRY

A Tarot spread is a way of laying out the cards to do a reading. There are hundreds of Tarot spreads out there for you to try and each one has a different energy. There are new ones being invented all the time – and there is nothing to stop you from inventing your own if you so desire. Even with the most popular, or oldest, spreads the positions and meanings are not set in stone and you will find that Tarot readers often adjust parts of a famous spread so that it works for them.

THE CELTIC CROSS

The Celtic Cross is the most widely used Tarot spread and is often the one that is suggested in the little white book that comes with a deck of cards. It has two sections: the cross on the left and the staff on the right (see p.118).

The cross is concerned with what is going on in the present. The two cards that form the middle cross symbolize you and what is "crossing" you. Around them in a circle are cards that show what is influencing this situation: what's behind you, what's in front of you, what's above you, what's below you. (Or, in simpler terms: past, future, what is on your mind, what is the root of the situation.)

The staff gives your question, or problem, a broader context. It looks at how attitudes (your own and other people's) affect the problem, and highlights your hopes and fears. The final card gives you a suggested outcome – or, as I often like to think of it, what is likely to happen if things continue in the way they are going right now (i.e. if you don't make any changes).

This is a spread that really rewards the reader for taking the time to search for a story. Sometimes, it takes several readings (and re-readings) of the cards to find it, but it will always be worth it in the end.

Try the Celtic Cross for yourself using the diagram on the next page. There's a sample reading after it for you to follow, too.

CELTIC CROSS SPREAD

- The most popular spread used by Tarot readers.
- Covers a lot of ground and gives a thorough discussion.
- Is adaptable for specific questions or more general readings.

Layout

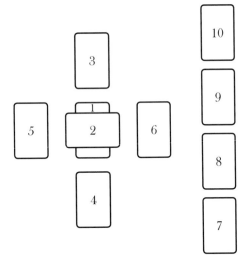

Key

1. You – the heart of the matter

2. What "crosses" or challenges you

3. Above you – what is on your mind

4. Below you – the root of the matter

5. Behind you – your immediate past

6. Before you – your immediate future

7. Your attitude to yourself

8. Others' attitudes to you – e.g. friends, family

9. Your hopes and fears

10. The outcome

SAMPLE READING

Toby's question

"I am feeling a bit swamped by all my commitments and responsibilities right now. How can I get my life more under control?"

Toby's reading

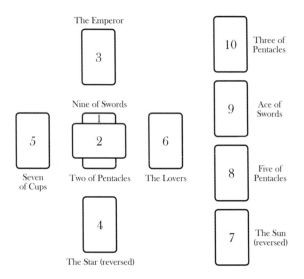

The Emperor — 3

Nine of Swords — 1

5 — Seven of Cups

2 — Two of Pentacles

6 — The Lovers

4 — The Star (reversed)

10 — Three of Pentacles

9 — Ace of Swords

8 — Five of Pentacles

7 — The Sun (reversed)

Breakdown

Toby has four cards from the major arcana and six from the minor arcana. This could show that his problems are mostly about the day-to-day managing of his life.

He has no cards from the suit of Wands, which could highlight his inability to use his own resources and energy to solve his problem.

He has two reversals, which seem to point to the areas of his life that need to be unblocked. In this case his self-doubt and the need to let more joy into his life.

Card by card

You – the Nine of Swords suggests negative feelings, depression and sleepless nights.

What crosses you – the Two of Pentacles is often about balancing finances.

What is on your mind – the Emperor shows a strong desire to achieve goals.

The root of the matter – the reversed Star card can point to feelings of self-doubt.

It is clear from Toby's question that he is suffering at the moment and this is backed up by the Nine of Swords that appears in the first position. What is causing this pain? The Two of Pentacles suggests that finances and the need to juggle them is presenting a challenge, but at the root of the matter are Toby's feelings of inadequacy and self-doubt. However, the Emperor shows his strong desire to get things under control.

Your immediate past – the Seven of Cups can point to having too many choices.

Your immediate future – the Lovers suggests an important choice needs to be made.

These cards make an interesting pair, as they are both about choices. It seems as though Toby has had decisions to make in the past – but his question tells us that he has not been making good ones or has been putting them off altogether and trying to do everything at once. The appearance of the Lovers in the immediate future tells us that he will not be able to do this for much longer.

Your attitude to yourself – the reversed Sun describes a need to let more joy into life.

Others' attitudes to you – the Five of Pentacles suggests a need for guidance.

It seems as though Toby is not allowing himself to have much fun at the moment and it is likely that his friends are aware of this. The Five of Pentacles may be telling Toby to turn to them for advice and help.

Your hopes and fears – the Ace of Swords can point to an uncomfortable truth.

The outcome – the Three of Pentacles shows someone working with skill and expertise.

It would appear that Toby is afraid of something – possibly something that he is refusing to admit to himself, which is causing his inability to make the choices necessary to take control of his life. However, the Three of Pentacles suggests that the situation is likely to resolve itself in a positive way, with Toby finding a way to put aside the self-doubt and concentrate on the things he is good at – with a little help from his friends.

HORSESHOE SPREAD

- Works well for specific questions or problems.
- Deal the cards in the shape of a horseshoe for extra luck.

Layout

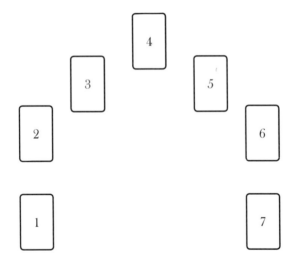

Key

1. Past events influencing the situation

2. Present events influencing the situation

3. Future events that will influence the situation

4. Your thoughts about the situation

5. Other influences on the situation

6. Obstacles to watch out for

7. The most likely outcome if nothing changes

ANNUAL FORECAST SPREAD

- Deal cards in a clockwise circle and use the cards to see what is in store for the coming year.
- Each card represents one month, with the first card dealt representing the current month.
- Try this spread on a meaningful day (for example, January 1 or your birthday), then make a note of the cards and look at them on the same date next year.

Layout

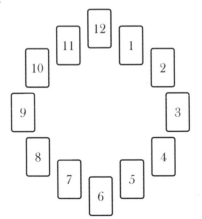

Key

1. Current month (e.g. January)
2. February
3. March
4. April
5. May
6. June
7. July
8. August
9. September
10. October
11. November
12. December

PENTAGRAM SPREAD

- Puts you in the centre of the reading – literally.
  (The five cards form a pentagram, or five-pointed
  star, around the centre card, which represents you.)

Layout

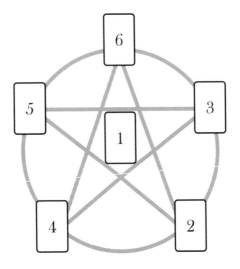

Key

1. You
2. Earth – what grounds you?
3. Air – what inspires you?
4. Fire – what challenges you?
5. Water – what are you learning?
6. Spirit – the outcome

PYRAMID SPREAD

- Useful when you want an in-depth reading, as it is more concerned with reflecting life than answering questions.

- Cards are read in rows rather than singly, so look for patterns and connections between the cards, using the tips in Part 4.

Layout

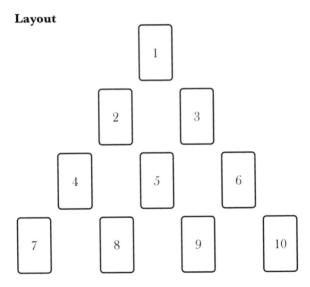

Key

1. Your life as it is now

2. 3. The lessons you are learning

4. 5. 6. Your current beliefs

7. 8. 9. 10. Your foundations (what you are building on)

EXTRA RESOURCES

There are many other spreads that you can use, which can be found either on the internet or in other books. Don't be surprised to find many variations on all the popular spreads. Check out the spreads suggested by the Labyrinthos Academy at: www.labyrinthos.co/pages/tarot-spreads-list.

If none of them quite answer the questions that you want to ask, you could even make up a spread of your own. You will find some great tips on how to start from the Llewellyn website: www.llewellyn.com.

As you feel more confident in your knowledge of the Tarot, you can use the cards to enhance other areas of your life, such as to help you set goals, discover more about yourself and connect with other people in your life.

PART 5

A MYSTIC LIFE

FIND YOUR POWER CARD

Further your journey into the world of Tarot magic by finding your power card. This is the card from the major arcana that is connected to your birthday and it contains wisdom that can help guide you at times when you doubt yourself. Here's how to do it:

Take the day, month and year of your birthday and add the numbers together until you have a number of 21 or less.

For example:
19/05/1976
1+9+5+1+9+7+6 = 38
3+8 = 11
Card 11 of the major arcana = Justice (p.38)

Simple. Take time to research the positive and negative aspects of your power card so that you can really explore its potential. You can draw on its power at times when you need encouragement or advice.

BRING LOVE INTO YOUR LIFE

This is a ritual to perform at night, before you go to bed. The spell sends a positive message out into the universe to attract the right kind of love you need.

Try this:

1. Create a sacred space and fill it with symbols of love. (If you don't know where to start, a shoebox wrapped in a silk scarf makes a great portable altar. Traditional symbols are fresh flowers, gems such as rose quartz and meaningful photos or pictures from magazines.)

2. Light a red candle to symbolize love and a white candle to signify the purity of your intent.

3. Pick a card from the pack that represents you and another to represent the kind of person you are looking for. (Court cards are great for this. Look back at the characters described in Part 2, and see which ones match you and the person you are looking for.)

4. Write down the things you are looking for in a partner and the activities, interests and emotions you want to share.

5. Place the two cards either side of the Two of Cups.

6. Imagine the people on the cards embracing and love flowing from one to the other.

7. Now imagine that love flowing out of the cards and into the universe.

8. To complete the ritual, say aloud, "I ask this with the purest of motivations" and blow out the candles.

9. Tuck the cards into a plain white or red envelope, alongside the paper you wrote on in step 4. Sleep with it by your bed and think about the cards as you go to sleep.

COUPLE GOALS

Try this reading with your partner and have fun opening new lines of communication. You may be surprised at what you find out.

Layout

Your cards	**Your partner's cards**
1	6
2	7
3	8
4	9
5	10

Key

1. You
2. Your emotions
3. Your desires
4. Your issues
5. Your goals

6. Your partner
7. Your partner's emotions
8. Your partner's desires
9. Your partner's issues
10. Your partner's goals

1. Sit opposite your partner and take turns shuffling the cards.

2. Split the deck roughly in half. Keep one half and give the other to your partner.

3. Deal a vertical line of five cards face down in front of you.

4. Ask your partner to deal a vertical line of five cards face down beside it.

5. Read the cards together, in pairs. (For example: you turn over your first card, then your partner turns over their first card.)

MEND A BROKEN HEART

These three spreads use the darkest cards of the Tarot to help you when you need it most. Create a focus for each reading by placing the major arcana that governs each spread first.

THE TOWER'S SPREAD: FIND YOUR STRENGTH

Layout

 　1　　2　　3　　4

Key

1. Your greatest strength
2. How to enhance this strength
3. How to apply this strength
4. What this strength brings you

DEATH'S SPREAD: TIME TO CHANGE

Layout

| 1 | 2 | 3 | 4 |

Key

1. Where you are now

2. What you need to lose

3. What you stand to gain

4. Future outcome

JUDGEMENT'S SPREAD: PROCESS PAINFUL MEMORIES

Layout

| 1 | 2 | 3 | 4 |

Key

1. Past issues
2. How to judge them
3. How to forgive them
4. Future outcome

SAMPLE READING

Helena's question

"My marriage has hit a rocky patch and my husband blames me. How can I make things better?"

Helena's reading

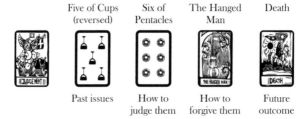

	Five of Cups (reversed)	Six of Pentacles	The Hanged Man	Death
	Past issues	How to judge them	How to forgive them	Future outcome

Card by card

Past issues – the Five of Cups is reversed to show trust issues or separation.

How to judge them – the Six of Pentacles is a card of generosity and sharing.

How to forgive them – the Hanged Man tells you to look at life from a different angle.

Future outcome – Death warns of an ending and a beginning.

Overall reading

It seems as though Helena and her husband have problems trusting each other, possibly after a past separation. Issues arising from this time have not been resolved between them. In order to move on, they will both need to be very understanding, sharing the blame equally and agreeing to move forward together. Have they really considered how each other feels? It would appear that it is time for a new cycle in their lives to begin.

ATTRACT WEALTH

Don't be afraid of abundance. Use the suit of Pentacles to perform a spell to increase wealth into your life.

Try this:

1. Sit somewhere you won't be disturbed and lay all the cards from the suit of Pentacles face up in a circle.

2. Light a green candle to symbolize abundance.

3. Look deeply into the flame and tell it your monetary desires. Don't hold back – many people have a nagging idea that it's wrong to desire wealth, but if you believe you are not worthy of abundance, the universe will react accordingly.

4. Look at the circle of cards and choose the one that best suits what you want from your financial situation. Use the key on the next page to help you.

5. Turn the other cards face down and study your chosen card. Try to use as many senses as possible to access the image. Imagine that you can feel the edge of the coins with your fingers, hear the chink of coins... If this makes you feel uncomfortable,

you need to work on those feelings of allowing yourself abundance.

6. Blow out the candle and say these words to end the spell:

I call for money and money comes to me.
I call for money and money comes to me.
I call for money and money comes to me.
Money is good for me. So mote it be.*

*"So mote it be" is a ritual phrase that means "so must it be". If you prefer, you could use the word "amen" which is a similar declaration of affirmation.

These are the keywords for this exercise, to help you choose which Pentacles card to work with:

Ace – new business opportunity

Two – balancing your finances

Three – financial rewards for hard work

Four – inheritance

Five – an offer of financial help

Six – financial generosity

Seven – investments

Eight – promotion at work

Nine – good fortune

Ten – material comfort

Page – a gift of money

Knight – achieving financial goals

Queen – abundance

King – financial security

CONTACT YOUR GUARDIAN ANGELS

Bring light and love into your life by tuning in to the wisdom of your guardian angels. This ritual ends with a five-card reading to discover what messages they have for you.

Try this:

1. Find a quiet space where you can relax and concentrate.

2. Light a white candle to represent the purity of your intentions.

3. Shut your eyes and let your mind drift as you recall the important events that have shaped your life, both good and bad.

4. Slow your breathing and, as you achieve a meditative state, thank your angels silently for being there for you at these times.

5. Imagine a clear space for your angels to appear in – maybe a white cloud, a stretch of beach or a sunlit room.

6. Ask your angels to meet you here. In some cases, you will be able to imagine the angels' physical shapes, but you may hear voices or just get a feeling of warmth and reassurance.

7. Relax into this feeling and ask the angels' permission to do the reading. If you don't feel safe and secure at this point, you can leave this reading for another time, or you can go back to stage 4 and try again.

8. Thank the angels and smile as you open your eyes. You are now ready to shuffle the deck and deal out five cards.

Layout

1	2	3	4	5

Key

1. Message about your love life

2. Message about your spiritual life

3. Message about your health

4. Message about your work life

5. What your angels want you to know right now

INTERPRET DREAMS

Although the contents of your dreams often seem silly, funny or just too random for your waking mind to explain, the Tarot can help you look for meaning. It is a great translator, because it speaks the same symbolic language as the subconscious.

Try this:

Find a quiet spot and picture or jot down the images you can recall from the dream. Then deal four cards in a row and read them from left to right.

Layout

Key

1. What subconscious thoughts have inspired the dream?
2. What recent life events have influenced the dream?
3. What is the dream really about?
4. What message does the dream have for you?

DISCOVER YOUR PAST LIFE

Use your cards to reveal how your past lives are affecting your current situation. Repeated patterns of behaviour or inexplicable fears in the present could have a karmic root. The final three cards in the reading (8, 9 and 10) suggest ways to help you heal your spirit and move forward.

Try this:

Shuffle the deck, then deal the cards, as follows.

Layout

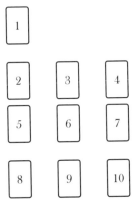

Key

1. Who you are now
2. Past life connections to education
3. Past life connections to your relationships
4. Past life connections to emotional wellbeing
5. Past life connections to destructive issues
6. Past life connections to money
7. Past life ties to your parents
8. Advice for healing past
9. Advice for healing present
10. Advice for healing future

CLEANSE YOUR CHAKRAS

Chakras are the invisible energy centres of your body. Seven main chakras run from the base of your spine to the crown of your head, each with a different physical and emotional significance.

Key	Chakra		Significance
1	Crown		Higher purpose
2	Third Eye		Wisdom
3	Throat		Communication
4	Heart		Compassion
5	Solar Plexus		Personal power
6	Sacral		Emotion
7	Root		Foundation

Try this:

Use this reading to see which chakras are balanced and which need work. Deal as many cards as you like in each of the seven positions, depending on how much information you feel you need. (For example, if you deal The Sun (p.54) in the first position, this is a very positive card and you will not be experiencing blocks here. Move on to the next one.)

Layout

```
┌─────┐
│  1  │
└─────┘

┌─────┐
│  2  │
└─────┘

┌─────┐
│  3  │
└─────┘

┌─────┐
│  4  │
└─────┘

┌─────┐
│  5  │
└─────┘

┌─────┐
│  6  │
└─────┘

┌─────┐
│  7  │
└─────┘
```

ESTABLISH TIMING

The suits of the minor arcana are associated with the four seasons:

Wands – spring
Cups – summer
Pentacles – autumn
Swords – winter

If you are asking questions that demand a timeframe and are getting a lot of cards from one suit then the Tarot might be giving you a hint. However, if you need more specific timings there are 12 cards that relate to specific times of the year, thanks to their associations with the zodiac.

Dates	Zodiac sign	Card
21 March–20 April	Aries	The Emperor
21 April–21 May	Taurus	The Hierophant
22 May–21 June	Gemini	The Lovers
22 June–22 July	Cancer	The Chariot
23 July–22 August	Leo	Strength
23 August–23 September	Virgo	The Hermit
24 September–23 October	Libra	Justice
24 October–22 November	Scorpio	Death
23 November–21 December	Sagittarius	Temperance
22 December–20 January	Capricorn	The Devil
21 January–19 February	Aquarius	The Star
20 February–20 March	Pisces	The Moon

Try this:

1. Take the 12 "zodiac" cards out of the deck.

2. Shuffle them, then spread them out face down in front of you.

3. Think about a reading you have just completed, or the events that you want a timeframe for.

4. Pick the card you are most drawn to. Turn it over and use the list to find out the dates it corresponds to. (Don't add the divinatory meaning of the card to this.)

A WORD OF WARNING

If you focus too hard on working out timing, you could miss out on what the cards are really trying to tell you. Tarot cards definitely lend themselves to a more narrative style of reading. If you ask them, "When will I meet my soulmate?" your answer won't be "Next Tuesday", however much you wish it were. Instead, the cards are more likely to have answers that start a dialogue, such as "When you learn to improve your communication skills" or "When you stop feeling bitter about past failures".

END NOTE

IS THE OUTCOME FIXED?

I hope you have enjoyed this introduction to these amazing cards, and that you have been inspired to get out there and start reading them. There is a wealth of information, in print and online, to help you delve more deeply into the world of Tarot and continue your journey.

Here are three websites to get you started:

- https://marykgreer.com – Mary K. Greer has written many fantastic books about detailed aspects of the Tarot and keeps an updated blog.

- www.aeclectic.net – for illustrated reviews of hundreds of inspiring cards, search the A–Z of Tarot decks.

- www.free-tarot-reading.net – this website provides free digital readings – handy for those times you have forgotten to bring your cards with you.

No reading is set in stone and the future is always changing. If you see a negative future then be thankful for the insight and change your actions accordingly. The cards are not "fortune tellers" and they don't cause events to happen – no matter what the movies want us to believe (I'm looking at you, James Bond!). Never let the cards create your reality. It's your life, and you can change the energies around you by changing your attitudes and choices.

THE LITTLE BOOK OF SPELLS

Astrid Carvel

ISBN: 978-1-78685-799-6

Paperback

£6.99

Discover the techniques for performing white witchcraft with this beginner's guide to casting spells. Learn the importance of the moon's cycles and ways to tap into the rhythms of the natural world, and how to source your own ingredients. From love potions using candle magic and rituals for attracting prosperity, to charm bags for courage and incantations for lasting happiness, there is a spell for every occasion.

If you're interested in finding out more about our books, find us on Facebook at **Summersdale Publishers** and follow us on Twitter at **@Summersdale**.

WWW.SUMMERSDALE.COM